BRITAIN IN OLD PHC

PORTSLADE

JUDY MIDDLETON

SUTTON PUBLISHING LIMITED

Sutton Publishing Limited
Phoenix Mill · Thrupp · Stroud
Gloucestershire · GL5 2BU

First published 1997

Copyright © Judy Middleton, 1997

Title page: Brewery workers in North Lane.

British Library Cataloguing in Publication Data
A catalogue record for this book is available from the
British Library.

ISBN 0-7509-1460-2

Typeset in 10/12 Perpetua.
Typesetting and origination by
Sutton Publishing Limited.
Printed in Great Britain by
Ebenezer Baylis, Worcester.

CONTENTS

Dear
      J have no face to tell you all that
happens in Portslade.

This delightful postcard dates from 1908. It was printed in colour, the lady wearing a burgundy coloured skirt and matching trimming on her hat. Her petticoat is on display and so is her ankle – a restrained version of a saucy postcard. One of the early English films made by local pioneer George Albert Smith features an inquisitive man out with his telescope who focuses on the ankle of a lady cyclist who has paused to do up her shoelace.

INTRODUCTION

It could be said that Portslade is a microcosm of Sussex. In other words, many features that are typical of Sussex can be found in the one place. For instance, there is the seashore with its ancient association with fishing; the canal and the industrial sites of the old gas works and electricity works, plus the merchant vessels bringing in wine and timber; moving northwards, there were the brickfields and places where sand and flints were extracted; then the valley area of rich earth where market gardens flourished; and finally the rolling chalk Downs, once populated with sheep.

In 1801 the population of Portslade was 284, whereas neighbouring Hove could only muster 101 people. Aldrington had nobody at all, while Hangleton and West Blatchington were downland hamlets with about 30 to 40 people each. This reflects accurately Portslade's position for many years as the most important parish of the five. There was also the acreage, of course, as Portslade had 2,780 acres, whereas the original limits of Hove stretched to 778 acres. It was the nineteenth century that tipped the balance and Hove began to expand rapidly. This culminated with Portslade being amalgamated with Hove in 1974. The action was not a thunderbolt from the blue, as the idea had been discussed at least since the 1930s and recommended in 1947.

The Brighton foot beagles with the master, Mr Ashby, leading the way up the High Street, 4 December 1928. The Southdown foxhounds also used to meet at Portslade. The occupants of North House Farm would greet them with glasses of cherry brandy. Meanwhile, young farmworker Francis Sclater would have scoured the Downs looking for foxes' earths and blocking them up. He earned 10s for each one.

THE OLD VILLAGE

When the Revd T.W. Horsfield came to write his two-volume work on Sussex in 1835, he was unimpressed by Hove but was most enthusiastic about Portslade. He wrote that the village was 'delightfully situated in a declivity of the Downs and sheltered by their height. The views of the sea are enchanting.' There is no doubt that it was a picturesque spot and, unlike Hove, the nearby slopes were well endowed with trees.

Although it was surrounded by wide open spaces, the village was densely populated. There were more rows of little flint cottages like Robin's Row. For instance, Hangleton Court at the east end of the High Street had around eleven cottages and the back wall is still extant as the high wall bordering the church twitten. There were other cottages too, like Fraser's Court tucked away behind the George inn. Some of these dwellings had their own wells close at hand, but there was a communal well in the village. Outside privies were constructed in rows at the bottom of gardens and, as there were only partitions separating them, it was quite possible for neighbours to hold a conversation while engaged in other business.

A charming portrait of Portslade village in 1840 by Henry Earp senior. It appears that Earp must have painted this at a later date, relying on sketches made by other members of the family, since he was born in 1830. One surprising aspect is the lack of trees in the foreground, but it does reflect the lovely downland setting. On the left is the imposing structure of Portslade House, which faced east across the valley.

This peaceful, sun-drenched view dates to the 1870s, before the new brewery was built. On the left is the small building with a thatched roof popularly known as the Hook and Eye. Next door is the George pub, as it was before being rebuilt. On the right is The Grange with a bricked-up window showing prominently in the west wall. Perhaps the owners of Portslade House objected to being overlooked.

The Grange is more prominent in this view of *c.* 1912. The garden wall is dark with cypress trees, probably planted in the 1860s when an extension was built at the back of the house. The garden also boasted a fig tree and a walnut tree. The house was demolished in about 1927. In the background is a rare glimpse of Hangleton Court, where E. Zwartouw & Sons, bakers, lived at no. 11 in 1902. These cottages were demolished in about 1914.

The brewery was taken over by Smithers & Sons in 1919, who soon dispensed with the distinctive steep-gabled roof by putting in an extra storey. The brickwork still looks new and raw in this view. It is plain to see what an impact the new brewery had on the character of the village, but the old buildings remain much as they were in the 1870s, except that the Hook and Eye has lost its thatch.

The George inn, 1880s. Behind the strange ecclesiastical-style windows was the long bar, and behind that was the smoking room. The premises were somewhat cramped, but in 1851 George Peters managed to live there with his wife, six children and two servants. He was also a cow-keeper. Indeed, it was traditional for the landlord of the George to earn his living by other means too.

One of the best known landlords of the George inn was Isaac Holland, mine host from 1887 until his death in 1908. He was also a builder, plumber, painter, wheelwright, undertaker, farrier and general smith. Such industry enabled him to become a property owner, and in 1903 he purchased the grocery shop next door and Fraser's Court nearby. In this picture of c. 1905, Isaac Holland is on the right by the cart. The large man is the blacksmith, Mr Humphreys.

It was not only the landlord of the George who followed multiple trades. Thomas Smith, landlord of the Stag's Head in the 1890s, was also a carpenter and joiner. This view of the early 1900s shows the original entrance. One regular was old Burt West, the shepherd, who came down for his weekly shopping and a drink. If his money ran out he would happily oblige with his party trick for a free pint – this involved biting off the head of a live rat.

Today's customers at the Stag's Head would be amazed at the number of entrances that used to punctuate the building in former days. The main entrance has been blocked up and transformed into a small window, while the bottle and jug department on the left has been turned into a larger window. The door on the far left (now the entrance to the saloon bar) led to a private cottage. In *c.* 1959 the Stag's Head was enlarged to include this property.

The bridge arching over the High Street was a favourite subject for picture postcards. It joined the two parts of the Portslade House property but it was not the first bridge there. The original one burned down in 1885. The fire was caused by sparks from a steamroller labouring up the incline. In August 1920 a group of infants from St Nicolas's Sunday school enjoyed an afternoon treat in the grounds, the highlight being when they were allowed to stand on the bridge.

A later view of the bridge with the Broomfield brothers standing in the foreground. On the left is John, wearing the uniform of Hove High School, and on the right is Peter, who had recently joined the Royal Navy. At this time the Broomfields were still farming extensively in the area. Note the breach in the flint wall, made to build the properties in High Close, the plans for which were approved in 1936.

In neither of the two previous views is the steepness of the hill really apparent. However, the gradient was obviously too much for this steamroller, which overturned on 8 April 1914. It must have been a spectacular crash as the vehicle weighed ten tons and the noise obviously brought the neighbours running, with the local photographer hot on their heels. It was an Edison steamroller with an Aveling Porter engine.

The village looks strangely deserted in this view. In the background are the properties known as the Swiss Cottages. In 1923 they were up for sale as part of the Portslade Farm estate and they were described as an old-fashioned pair of cottages, brick and flint built, rough cast and tile-healed. The rent was 3s 6d a week each and there was a strip of garden. The cottages survived until the 1960s.

A drawing of Fraser's Court, 1920s. These cottages were situated on the north side of the High Street and were reached by a narrow twitten between the shop next door to the George inn and a private cottage. There were nine cottages of the two-up-and-two-down variety arranged around a brick and cobbled yard, with a row of seven outside privies in the north-west corner. The name may derive from Ellen Fraser, who was the owner from 1887 until 1900 and was John Dudney's sister.

Daisy Ford outside one of Freeman's Court cottages, 1920s. These cottages were at Southern Cross on the west side of Locks Hill and were built in two blocks, one facing Locks Hill and the other fronting the Old Shoreham Road (the latter later obscured by Tate's Garage). In 1861 there were forty-eight people living at Freeman's Court, mostly labourers, but a blacksmith and a shepherd too.

Right: Robin's Row, *c.* 1740. The name Robin's Row goes back at least to the 1840s. Curiously, the neighbouring block was built at a right angle to it, making for rather cramped access to the front doors. However, this is how much of old Portslade must have looked: cheek by jowl. In 1881 this group of five flint cottages contained twenty-two souls, but this was spacious living compared with previous years. In 1895 the rent was 3*s* 2*d* a week.

Below: A wonderfully evocative study of Read's Supply Stores, *c.* 1910. Hector Read ran the business at 56 High Street and lived next door at no. 58. By 1910 he had branched out to Southern Cross (as the advertising states), where he had a shop at 78 Trafalgar Road. Hector kept the horse round the back, where its stable still survives. So too does a brick in the garden, where Hector scratched his name and the date 1900.

What strikes you about this picture is the empty road together with the number of trees. However, there are many other points worth noting. On the left is the private field (later to become the village green), then Lindfield House (demolished in 1961) and, in the distance, Portslade Farm House. The word Lindfield arose from the family that owned the land in the eighteenth century. The house was built in the 1860s for William Dudney of the brewery family, and here he lived with his wife Fanny, two sons and four daughters.

THE BREWERY

John Dudney was born at Shermanbury, Sussex in 1810. He moved to Portslade with his family in 1849 after living at Henfield for some years. He started his brewery business in a very small way, employing just two men in 1851. Twenty years later there were thirteen men working at the brewery. When Dudney was seventy years old he decided on a grand scheme of expansion. During the years he had acquired various plots of land, including a spring, cottages and the Stag's Head. When the malt tax was repealed in 1880, it seemed like a good time to forge ahead. The huge new brewery was erected, towering over the neighbouring cottages like a yellow-brick monolith. Having achieved what he set out to do, Dudney seemed content to sell his business to the Mews brothers in 1884. Dudney lived on to the grand age of eighty-five. He was buried in Portslade cemetery under a slab-like stone.

A Victorian journalist writing in 1882 described in flowery language the man and his business enterprise: 'Unknown to all but John Dudney, who is an archaeologist, Portslade has a spring of rare water, and he, in his amateur efforts at brewing . . . discovering in this water elements of excellence beyond those of neighbouring streams, directed the friendly tributary, flowing in unseen courses, unto himself.'

This view dates to the 1880s, when John Rich was landlord of the Stag's Head, as can be seen from the sign. In 1878 the Stag's Head was purchased by John Dudney. On 8 April 1884, in two separate transactions, the Dudney family sold to the Mews brothers the Stag's Head and cottage, the Victoria Hotel, Portslade, plus property in Hove and Worthing for £6,700, while the brewery itself went for a staggering £170,000.

Both of these illustrations date from 1891. The top one shows the fermenting room, which measured 96 feet by 42 feet and contained eleven fermenting vessels, some made of pinewood and others constructed of slate, but each holding 50 barrels. The walls were painted white and the ironwork was red. The windows were fitted with wire-woven outside blinds to shield the vessels from the heat of the sun. The bottom picture shows the racking room, which measured 96 feet by 55 feet. As well as housing around a hundred vessels, it also contained the yeast press and the yeast store. The brewery was one of the largest in the South. The water from the well was pumped up at the rate of 10,000 gallons an hour and stored in a reservoir at the top of the building. The well was always understood to be 100 feet deep, but when Smithers took over it was discovered to be only 87 feet.

Left: The malthouse in Drove Road is the only one still surviving in the Hove and Portslade area. It is probable that it was built around the same time as the new brewery, but it is also possible that it dates from the time of the old brewery workings and was re-roofed in the 1890s. At any rate it is now a Grade II listed building. The projection on the left housed a steam-directed hoist, which lifted the malt from the wagons parked directly underneath. Below: The building featured here was Dudney's original brewery. By 1891 it contained the ale, wine and spirit stores, having direct communication with the main building by the iron bridge on the left. Underneath the bottling stores were the beer cellars, some 70 feet long and containing ten arches. On the north side was the room where the spirits were stored in huge casks. The casks and barrels were made by the brewery's own cooperage department.

In 1898 Portslade Council approved plans submitted by Messrs Mews for twelve houses in North Lane (now North Road) to accommodate brewery workers. Each house also had an allotment of sixteen rods so that employees could grow their own vegetables. The properties were basically the first modern development north of the old village area. Before that the land was in agricultural use, but it was auctioned in 1895 and purchased by the Mews brothers.

As can be seen from this and the above view of North Lane, the hard working brewery workers produced numerous children. The company certainly attracted loyal staff, and Philip Packham, head brewer, stayed for fifty-one years. In 1910 there was a John Packham at 7 North Lane and an Alfred Packham at no. 12. Another long-standing employee was the splendidly named Edward Sebastopol Jupp, who, as copperside boy, boiled wort for the first brew in 1882 and was still working in 1936.

The base of the tall chimney belonging to the brewery, 1973. This view shows the splendid Victorian carving of bunches of grapes and ears of barley, with a shield bearing the initials D & S (Dudney and Son) and the date 1881. Although nothing could be more utilitarian than a brewery, Dudney obviously enjoyed these little architectural flourishes. Another embellishment is the frieze of Tudor-style roses under the old roofline.

Smithers took over the brewery in 1919. An extra storey was added, the well was extended to a depth of 249 feet and these lorries were used to ferry 'best bottled beers' to the customers. Yet it had not been so many years since the brewery had boasted its own stables with eighteen stalls and three loose boxes, a special room for drying the horses' harness and its own shoeing forge.

ST NICOLAS'S CHURCH

S t Nicolas's Church is the only church in the Hove and Portslade area that has been in continuous use since its foundation in about 1170. By the nineteenth century the ancient churches of Aldrington, Hove, Hangleton and West Blatchington were either reduced to a heap of ruins or in an advanced state of decay. However, Portslade's church kept its fabric intact because, out of the five parishes, it had the largest acreage and supported a higher population. Then too, the proximity of the manor and the interest of its occupants must have been an important factor.

The original church was a simple structure containing a nave and a south aisle, and it was built of flints with Caen stone dressings. It must have been somewhat gloomy inside as the windows we see today were later additions. However, it was solidly constructed and the two massive pillars in the south aisle still help to support the structure more than 800 years later.

It is quite possible that there was an earlier church on the same site. Indeed, it is more than likely that this was a sacred place going back into the mists of time. Gregory I, consecrated pope in 590, had a particular interest in converting England to Christianity and his advice was to build churches on sites that already held special significance for the people.

This beautiful scene, looking west from the grounds of Portslade Manor, was drawn in 1837. The people of the manor had their own private doorway leading into the churchyard and the paved pathway shows the way. Once inside the church the family would have sat in splendid isolation in their own manor pew.

The great interest in this drawing is not necessarily the church because it also shows the old Portslade Manor in the background. Depictions of the latter are few and far between. In fact, at present the only other known example is in the Sharpe collection. The two buildings were so close that part of today's churchyard wall was once part of the manor's fabric. Both relied heavily on flint in their construction.

This drawing is by the well-known artist R.H. Nibbs. Note particularly the absence of the manor in the background. Does this mean that the building had been demolished by then, was it not visible from his viewpoint, or did the artist not wish to include it in his sketch? An interesting detail is the little staircase, which used to lead to the old choir gallery.

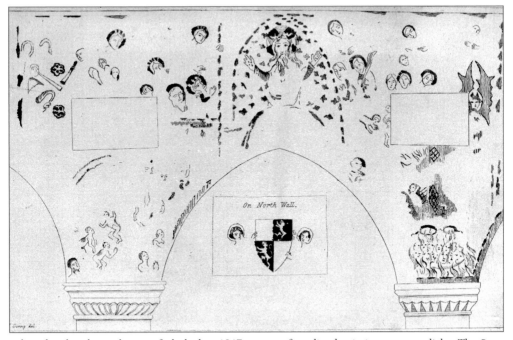

When the church was being refurbished in 1847, traces of medieval paintings came to light. The *Doom* painting or *Last Judgement* was not an unusual subject, but its position on the south wall of the nave was uncommon. The sinners roast in flames above the south-west pillar while the just ascend to heaven from the south-east pillar. After the drawing was made, lime wash was sloshed over the walls and the paintings were obliterated.

This view shows another interesting aspect of the church. The chancel can clearly be seen together with its three windows, but one is lower than the others. This feature is popularly known as a low side window, although the reason for its creation is still a puzzle. The most appealing explanation is that it enabled lepers to see Mass being celebrated from outside. A more prosaic one is that it was an unglazed opening through which the bell was rung.

The ivy began to take hold on the church tower in the 1850s (see Nibbs' drawing on p. 25). By the time of this view in about 1906, the ivy was at its most luxuriant. The Victorians thought the dark evergreen added a certain grandeur and mystery to old buildings, but it probably did little to help the fabric. Note the flourishing row of sycamores growing over the tumbled ruins of the manor.

Above: You could say this building looks the same today as it did in the 1950s. Indeed it does. However, the roofline is imperceptibly higher. This is because, when major repairs were undertaken in the 1980s, it was found that the Horsham slabs had not been laid with enough overlap to give a watertight seal. It meant more Horsham slabs and a steel truss inside the walls to support the extra weight.

Right: The church tower viewed from the twitten, 1950s. The tower was built in two stages, the lower portion being completed in about 1250 while the battlemented top was not added until the late fourteenth century. The tower contains three tenor bells, the earliest cast before 1529. Some branches of apple blossom rise above the wall of the vicarage garden, part of which was later sacrificed to construct the church hall and car park.

These two Buckoll tombstones are remarkable for their beautiful simple lettering, so that the inscriptions are as clear today as when the stonemason laid down his tools. John Buckoll was a tailor. He must have made a good living because when he died he left property to his family, including a house, outhouses, a stable and a garden. The family must have fallen on hard times later as, in the 1770s, a Dame Buckoll was receiving assistance from the parish.

These two tombstones are sited near the Buckoll pair, but they are completely different in lettering style and decorative motifs. Most people would find the cherubs' heads more cheerful to contemplate than the coffin and skulls of the Buckoll stones. The rectangular stone is in memory of Sarah Michell, who died in 1776. She is described as the 'relict' of her husband – an old-fashioned word for a widow, derived from the Latin verb 'to leave behind'.

William Kerr was a veteran of the Battle of Waterloo who died in 1854, aged seventy-five. He spent eighteen years as a private in the 12th Light Dragoons, serving in Egypt, Spain and Flanders, and then he returned to spend thirty-six peaceful years in Portslade. Technically he was a Chelsea pensioner because his Army pension was paid from the Chelsea Royal Hospital. How his tales of foreign places must have enthralled the locals, most of whom had never ventured outside Sussex.

This tombstone has a fragmented inscription in Norwegian and is in memory of Bernt Nikolai Olsen, captain of the brigantine *Rederinden* from Ostteroseer in Norway. It also serves as an object lesson to the local historian not to jump to conclusions, because the unfortunate captain was not drowned in a storm at sea; he was killed by getting out of the train on the wrong side at Portslade station, straight into the path of the Brighton express.

There could not be a greater contrast to the somewhat austere interior of the church than the opulence of the Brackenbury Chapel. Here there is an abundance of stained glass, marble, carved oak, sculptured stone and lovely floor tiles. It was erected in 1869 for the Brackenbury family, whose ancestors came over with William the Conqueror. Hannah Brackenbury's two brothers and a niece had died, leaving her an extremely wealthy woman. It is estimated that she gave away at least £100,000 during her lifetime and there were more bequests at her death. The family motto is in the chapel: 'Sans recueller jamais' (without ever drawing back).

In about 1250 the chancel was built. It has a slight inclination to the south. This feature is popularly called a weeping chancel as it represents Christ's head bowed on the cross. In the south wall the piscina and sedilia were constructed. The former was used to wash the vessels for Mass and the latter were seats for the celebrant and his assistants.

The sedilia is decorated at the foot of the hood mould by a head on either side. This is one of them. It may be a portrait of the parish priest of the time. It would be interesting to know if he was as independent as his predecessor, Stephen, who put Portslade on the map in 1185 by disputing who should receive the parish's tithes.

St Nicolas's bible class, 1913. The class members were standing in front of a charabanc, which was about to take them on an outing. The location is Trafalgar Road, and in the background is J.S. Hart's grocery (now the post office) and Frank Hart's butchers shop. There were several organizations connected with the church, including a coal club with eighty-seven members, where coal was purchased at cheaper summer prices. There was also a Band of Hope with a fife and drum band.

St Nicolas's Football Club, 1923/4 season. This picture was taken by A. Gundry, photographer, of 25 Eastbrook Road. The team played at Victoria Park, but social activities were based at St Nicolas's church hall in Abinger Road. In 1923 there was a men's club, a lads' club and a gym available every evening at the hall, while on Sundays there were lads' and girls' Bible classes – held separately, of course.

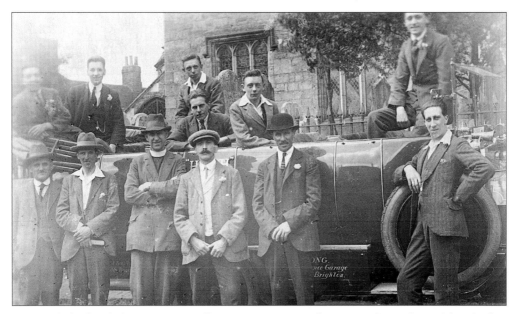

A St Nicolas's Church choir outing to Midhurst, 23 June 1925. The man standing in front of the wheel on the right is Perce Cranham, who also appears in the front row of the previous view. Standing at the back, third from the left, is Hector Coustick, while John Coustick leans on the bonnet. The vicar is the Revd Donald Campbell. In those days the choir consisted of eighteen men and boys, who dressed in black cassocks and white surplices for church services.

Parish mission, 1950s. Back row, left to right: Revd John Knight, Mrs Adams, Revd Ronald Adams, Sister Holland and Revd Peter Bide. In front is the parish mission team. Father Knight and Father Adams arrived in Portslade in 1948, while the diminutive Sister Holland was a Church Army lay worker. At that time the vicar of St Nicolas's Church was also responsible for the Good Shepherd and St Helen's Church, Hangleton.

The interior of the church, 4 November 1983. To the right of the chancel is the small stained glass of St Francis, put there in memory of the Revd Armstrong Boyle, who was vicar from 1899 until 1919. He was a man of liberal sympathies and supported the women's suffrage movement. He also recorded that nightingales sang in the vicarage garden. His first cousin, Lt-Cdr Edward Courtney Boyle, won the Victoria Cross in 1915 while in command of the submarine E14.

The Revd E.P.W. Holmes was vicar from 1933 to 1946, a particularly busy time with the Second World War adding extra work. He kept the church unlocked all day in case the air-raid sirens went off and people needed to shelter inside, while his wife Mary donned her tin hat and did her spell of firewatching at night. Many people will remember Mary as a redoubtable lay chairman of Hove Deanery Synod.

FARMS & OPEN SPACES

In the past, Portslade was a great place for farms. Now that it is so heavily built up, it is difficult to envisage its former rural aspect. Where the houses and traffic in the Valley Road area are today was once the domain of haystacks and horses, potatoes, carrots, sprouts and turnips, besides many blackcurrant and gooseberry bushes. Portslade Farm (the farmhouse next to Robin's Row) specialized in poultry and dairy-fed pork, and offered good pasture to horses requiring care and rest. There were many fine horses, too, at the famous Paddocks Racing Stables, and there were numerous sheep on the Downs.

As regards public open spaces, Portslade was a comparative latecomer. Victoria Recreation Ground was not opened until 1902, and Easthill Park was officially opened in 1948. In the 1930s there were great hopes that the grounds of Portslade House would become a public park, but unfortunately the opportunity was lost.

In later years Vale Park was laid out and Mile Oak Recreation Ground opened. Perhaps most surprising, Portslade has recently acquired two new open spaces: the Benfield Valley Park and the playground at Fox Way.

The only feature in this view of the 1920s that can still be seen today is the Foredown Water Tower. All of the rest – the Foredown Isolation Hospital, the farmhouses, the market gardens and the fields – have been swept away by a relentless tide of housing. North House Farm is the large building set among trees, while the Stonery is in front of it in the valley.

This view of farmland, although still including the farmhouses, swings towards the north and the undulating shape of the Downs. One aspect of the landscape that has proved remarkably durable is the old flint wall. It is surprising how often stretches of them have survived, a witness to old boundaries. If they still served a purpose they were left alone, while some flint walls, like the boundaries of St Nicolas's Churchyard, are part of a conservation area.

New England Farm, 1930s. This view makes the farm look somewhat remote in its downland setting. However, urban life is not too far away and the chimney belonging to the Brighton waterworks can just be seen on the left. Today the Brighton bypass sweeps across the site, but walkers can still reach the countryside beyond via an underpass, which comes out near a clump of trees.

New England Farm, looking north, 1920s. In 1881, when the census was being taken, the enumerator carefully noted that an agricultural labourer by the name of Samuel Denman was camped out in New England Barn. He was probably one of those independent labourers who moved from farm to farm, working where he was needed. A gale blew down this barn in c. 1900.

The four views of North House Farm on these two pages all date from the 1940s. Above is a flock of Southdown sheep close-folded. Note the continuing use of traditional materials in the woven hurdles and the barrel-shaped feeders. Mr Broomfield surveys the scene. At this time the Broomfields farmed extensively at Portslade – the Stonery, New England Farm and North House Farm – about 300 acres. Below is an area that for some reason was called north and south dungeon fields. Note the splendid haystacks thatched by Bert Hyde. These were allowed to settle for two weeks, then Bert set to work using straw rather than the reeds used for domestic dwellings. In 1944 a British bomber cushioned its crash by landing on top of one of Bert's haystacks. The crew survived.

The horses shown above were still a valuable asset during the 1940s, ploughing the land in the traditional way. This field is now covered by the grounds of Portslade Community College. The school was built originally as Portslade Senior Girls' School and it was the first serious dent in Broomfield's farmland. The need for a new school was one of the main reasons for issuing a compulsory purchase order. The picture below shows horse drilling. When old John Broomfield heard the news that some of his land would be taken away, he was angry and remarked to Bert Hyde: 'They want all this bally land from me.' Strong language, indeed, as 'bally' was the nearest he ever came to swearing. Although there were two Broomfields on the council, they could not vote on the issue because they had a vested interest.

The Stonery in the 1920s, when the land was farmed by the Broomfields. The property probably takes its name from the ubiquitous flint stones, which were so abundant that country folk thought they must grow. The Broomfields maintained that the Stonery was haunted by old Mother Godsmark, whose husband died in 1829. She wore a long gown and loose hair, and appeared during the winter.

In 1906 the Paddocks was taken over by Robert Price, who planned to turn the grounds into pleasure gardens with the help of his wife and daughters. This view dates from 1907, when he was just starting out on his enterprise. Visitors could inspect the Paddocks stables and enjoy tea in this secluded spot. However, if they wanted to visit at the weekend, they had to make sure it was a Saturday since no business was conducted on a Sunday.

The Paddocks in full swing as a pleasure ground. The 40 acres here provided ample space in which to play cricket, football, tennis, croquet, bowls and quoits. There was also the model farm to visit, besides the stables and an aviary. It was claimed that there was sufficient accommodation to give 500 visitors tea. For children there was a simpler diversion – sliding down a steep grass bank, popularly known as the tobogganing bank.

A group of jockeys at the Paddocks racing stables, c. 1914. Tommy Avery is on the left and the housekeeper, Molly Archer, stands in the centre. There is a strong local tradition that the 1908 Derby winner was trained here, but this does not appear to be backed up by official records. The horse in question was a bay filly called Signorinetta, a rank outsider that won at 100–1. She was bred, owned and trained at Newmarket by Cavaliere Odoardo Ginistrelli.

The old forge in Foredown Road, 1973. Shortly after, new housing obscured the view of the Downs in the distance. This is the last surviving forge in Portslade. At about the same time another old forge was being demolished at Southern Cross as part of the Old Shoreham Road widening scheme. Other forges were in the village, at the brewery and at Copperas Gap. In 1841 the blacksmith at the latter was Abraham Coom, while in 1851 Abel Coom worked in the same trade in the village.

At Foredown Road the Burgess family were working the forge for more than a hundred years (from 1849 until 1956): John Burgess (1822–1914) followed by his son Hugh Burgess (1875–1956). John Burgess was a tenant of the Borrer family, but in 1881 he purchased the forge for himself. Here, Hugh is at work, c. 1900.

The Brighton Waterworks, Mile Oak, 10 April 1929. This installation was prompted by the exceptionally dry years of 1890 to 1900. Although the Goldstone Pumping Station produced more water than other sources, it was thought prudent to look elsewhere too. The waterworks manager had his own spacious house nearby and there were also cottages for the workers.

The beautiful grounds of Easthill Park, 1950s. This land had only recently become a public park, having been opened in July 1948. Easthill House was built for the Blaker family in the 1840s, and in 1871, Edward Blaker, a landowner of 550 acres, lived here with his wife Emma, five children and servants, including a governess, cook, nurse and under-nurse. During the great gale of 16 October 1987, Easthill Park lost 160 mature trees.

Sunny Sunday afternoon at Victoria Recreation Ground, 2 December 1906. The only patrons appear to be two children on small, wheeled horses. How different this is from the scene at the grand opening on 11 August 1902, when there were 1,300 children taking part in the specially organized games. The event happily coincided with the coronation of Edward VII.

It is curious how many of Portslade's parks have been created on land rendered quite unfit for housing. For instance, Victoria Recreation Ground was once a brickfield, while its eastern extension was used as a rubbish dump. Vale Park was even more worked over, having been used for the extraction of sand and flint, then as a training ground for soldiers in the First World War, and finally the holes were filled up with refuse. The playground at Fox Way used to be a chalk-pit.

THE GAS WORKS &
THE CANAL

The gas works at Portslade were constructed in 1870–1 on a 7-acre site between the canal and the sea. In 1882 the two local gas companies amalgamated, and by 1885 gas making at Black Rock and on the site next door to St Andrew's Church, Hove, had ceased, all operations being transferred to Portslade. As the population increased, so did the demand for gas. Whereas in 1880 annual output had been 400 million cubic feet, by 1914 it had risen to 1,500 million cubic feet. More land and more plant capacity were required, and by 1926 the gas works occupied 40 acres.

The canal at Portslade was originally part of the River Adur, which by the eighteenth century ran into the sea at Wish Meadow, 3½ miles east of Shoreham. However, it rather lost its function in 1760 when the Shoreham Harbour Commissioners decided to make a cut through the shingle bank at Kingston, thus returning the harbour mouth closer to Shoreham. In 1851 the waterway was deepened and lock gates were erected. This enraged local merchants whose oyster beds were destroyed, but it set the seal on the canal becoming an important industrial site, soon to be confirmed by the arrival of the gas works.

An aerial view of the gas works, 1930s. On the left are the tar and storage tanks, while there are three retort houses ranged along the canal side and a line of purifiers stretch along the sea side. It certainly looks like an exposed site, and in 1875 the combination of gales and a high tide meant that the sea joined the canal, flooding the works to a depth of 18 inches.

This photograph shows one of the horses owned by the gas works, 1888. His name was Bobby. Note his companion dressed in stout working garb, which included the traditional tie under the knees. Bobby was obviously a great favourite, and the day before he was put to sleep on 30 August 1891, a photographer was summoned to take a farewell portrait of his head and shoulders to include in the company's archive.

Horses that are not properly looked after do not win prizes, so it is evident that those employed by the gas works received every attention. This was the scene on the Whit Monday Horse Parade on 30 May 1909, when the horses were the winners of the first prize. Horses were still in use during the Second World War, and in September 1940, when four bombs fell on the gas works, the only casualty was a horse.

In 1930 the gas company took over a neighbouring gas company, adopting a new title: the Brighton, Hove and Worthing Gas Company. Such a move required additional plant, including a 24-inch trunk main from Portslade to the Worthing holders. This view dates from 12 August 1931, when the ground was being excavated for foundations at no. 3 retort house. Note that horse power (in its original sense) was still a serious option.

This house, shown here on 3 January 1888, was where the foreman lived from 1870 until 1889. However, in 1890 it was demolished to make way for a new gantry at the west end of no. 2 retort house. Beach House was then constructed for the company's resident engineer. It was built on the edge of Portslade's boundary and, when an east wing was added, that portion was in Aldrington. Thus engineer C.H. Rutter used to joke that he and his wife slept in different parishes.

No. 2 wharf on an apparently windless day, 5 September 1889. Up until this time the gas works had relied on a single timber-built wharf. This new one was constructed in 1889. Although timber was still employed in the pitch-pine frame of piles, concrete was used for the wharf. However, progress was painfully slow because work could only go ahead at low tide for two hours at a time.

The gas works had its own fire brigade, quite independent of the Portslade division. Naturally there was some crossover. For example, Chief Officer Packer, who received his long service medal after ten years in the Gas Works Fire Brigade, had previously been Second Officer in the Portslade Fire Brigade. Here the men pose in front of one of the retort houses in May 1908.

The erosion of the beach from no. 2 groyne at the back of the gas works, 30 August 1933. This was perhaps not too surprising considering the prevailing shingle drift and the fact that the derrick in the background was used to hoist shingle from the beach for use as ballast. On the left but out of view were the beach cottages, originally huts dating from the First World War, but later occupied by gas works personnel.

Although the small ferry was once such a common sight, surprisingly few photographs of it have survived. The Portslade 'gassies', as they were called, were ferried back and forth every working day. It was by far the quickest route because if they walked it meant trudging all the way to the end of the canal at Aldrington and then along the coast.

Two ferry boats that were made at the gas works, 1 March 1934. The gas works employed a number of skilled craftsmen, including blacksmiths and carpenters. In the 1870s a carpenter at the works could earn £1 10s a week, which was a good wage compared with that of unskilled labourers in the St Barnabas area of Hove in 1881, who earned as little as 16s a week.

The SS *Petworth*'s first trip to the gas works, 30 August 1934. The adjacent ship is the *Pulborough*, which was launched on 7 August 1933 by Gladys Jones, daughter of one of the company's directors. The *Pulborough* was specially built to carry coal from the Tyne ports to Portslade, and it could transport 1,400 tons at a time. In 1933 it was stated that the works needed 160,000 tons a year to keep going.

A general view of the vertical plant at the gas works, 5 April 1954. In front is another coal ship, the *Seaford*, but this one could carry only 850 tons. An old sea dog with a long association with the company's vessels was Capt. W.O. Ginty. He joined the *Seaford* in 1918, having twice been torpedoed in the First World War. Ginty was promoted to master in 1924 and transferred to the *Pulborough* in 1934.

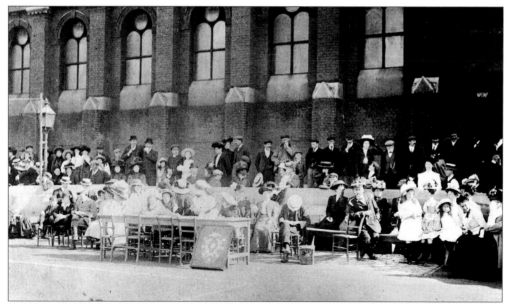

The gas works sports day, 1909. The company had its own recreation ground on site, and it was here that the annual inspection and sports day was held, an event that started in 1904. It was a great day out for the families, and the Portslade gassies were like a family, as many relatives worked together. For example, there were three generations of the Harmes family and three generations of the Candys, not to mention several members of the Mepham family.

The annual sports day was still going strong in 1914. The crowd is watching the drill of the gas works fire brigade. No doubt a highlight for the children and a worry for their parents was the trip across the canal on the ferry boat. In 1913 what was termed a 'laughable sketch' was staged on the day, called 'Weary Willie's Revenge'.

As well as providing employment, the gas works boasted a number of social activities. One of these was the cycle club. This was the heyday of cyclists, when groups could cycle out to the countryside in comparative peace, without feeling threatened by cars. By 1933 the works fielded its own cricket, football, bowls, and golf teams, and by 1935 there was a tennis team too.

The Gasco Rhythm Makers, 1940s. Seated at the piano is Fred Lucas senior, a man of ample proportions whose daytime job as the ferryman did little to slim his waistline. At one concert party he made a memorable impression by appearing as a Hawaiian maiden in a voluminous grass skirt. He also enjoyed playing the piano at the local pubs, the Clarence and the Windmill.

This postcard was posted on 14 June 1932 and shows the canal bank on the north side at the foot of Station Road. Just visible is the old Halfway House pub, supposedly sited midway between Shoreham and Brighton. In the past, harbour workers used to stage a race from the Halfway House to a pub in Shoreham carrying a 12 foot length of timber. Note also the painted ferry sign on the low building to the right.

The ferries in this and the previous view were for the use of ordinary members of the public. The canal looks as still as a millpond, but it is a deceptive calm because gusty weather could make this narrow stretch of water a dangerous place. On a Saturday evening in 1906, two young sisters, Florence and Mary Peters, were on a boating trip with their boyfriends when a sudden squall overturned the boat. The girls drowned.

A beautifully clear view of the canal bank, *c.* 1914. In the centre are the Britannia Flour Mills, with the spire of Our Lady, Star of the Sea, in the distance and the Crown inn on the right. Perhaps the greatest interest lies in the Star laundry on the left, run by Mr Miles, whose son Frederick G. Miles was destined to become a great name in British aviation. He built his first aircraft at the Star laundry.

F.G. Miles' first plane was a Gnat biplane, and he and Cecil Pashley, the pioneer pilot, started an aircraft business at Shoreham. In 1930 Miles moved to Reading, where he soon produced the Miles Hawk, the first monoplane to be mass-produced. This was followed by at least eight other designs, of which one was a Miles Falcon (winner of the King's Cup Air Race in 1935) and another the Miles Magister 1, shown here. The latter was a training aircraft much used by the RAF.

The famous Mystery Towers soared 180 feet above the canal, occupying the space where the power station was later built. They were designed by Sir Alexander Gibb as a sophisticated submarine barrier. The idea was to sink some concrete towers in the English Channel with nets and depth charges between them. In the event, only two were finished because work on them did not start until 1917 and peace was declared before others could be completed.

In 1920 one of the towers was carefully moved on the highest tide of the year and became the basis of the Nab Tower. Before it departed, visitors were allowed to land and climb to the top, and this is the view they saw. One sightseer was Mrs Marie Masters, who was seven months pregnant but still enthusiastically staggered to the top. However, when she saw how high up she was, she froze and had to be carried down.

RONUK

onuk was registered as trademark no. 192585 in 1896. The famous red polish started life as Fowler's Wax Composition – a somewhat uninspiring title. Thus a competition was held to find the best name, and Ronuk swept the board. There are two versions as to the derivation of the word: one source states that it was an Anglicized word suggested by an old Indian Army officer meaning brilliance; the other claimed that it was of Persian origin and signified the light on the edge of a well-tempered sword.

The Ronuk factory was established at Portslade in 1902, north of the railway line, its previous small premises having been at Providence Place, Brighton. When the factory was built, the surroundings were still rural, and older workers could remember an invasion of pigs from nearby fields. Indeed, in 1907 the management was moved to protest to the council about the piggeries.

The founder and managing director was Mr T. Horace Fowler, although it was his father who invented the polish. Mr Fowler was a model employer, providing all sorts of benefits for his employees, ranging from a staff savings fund (to provide for their old age) to a full-time welfare supervisor and a trained nurse. He also provided a 7-acre sports ground.

Here is a line-up of some of Ronuk's products in the 1930s. Taking pride of place in the centre is the famous floor polish. Originally, Fowler's Wax Composition was unscented and a nasty putty colour, but it evolved into a warm red polish with a distinctive smell. At one time Ronuk was used extensively on the floors of hospitals and schools up and down the country. Another product was furniture cream packaged in fine blue glass jars.

The interior of one of Ronuk's workshops, and the fearsome-looking machine in the foreground that produced tins for the polish. Later on the tins were produced by Barclay & Fry at Fishersgate, and latterly by the Metal Box Company at Portslade. In another workshop, Ronuk girls applied the lids after the tins were filled. The girls were so quick and skilled at whipping on the lids that a visitor in the 1930s, Lady Kate, compared it to sleight of hand.

A Ronuk delivery van. Note the royal coat of arms at the top. Ronuk was granted a royal warrant in 1907 by Edward VII, in 1910 by George V, in 1912 by Queen Alexandra and in 1940 by George VI. It is amusing to contrast the royal patronage with some other Ronuk uses. For example, it was once applied to the fuselage of aeroplanes and the hulls of racing ships to improve their speed.

Ronuk was of such importance that it merited its own railway sidings, which were constructed in 1919–20. By the 1950s the company tanker, which held 3,500 gallons, came direct to the sidings from Esso in Southampton Water. Beeswax was imported from several sources, including Rhodesia, while Benguellan wax came from the Congo and carnauba wax from Brazil.

The Duke and Duchess of York (later King George VI and Queen Elizabeth) visited Ronuk on 17 October 1924. At the time the Duke was president of the Industrial Welfare Society and the Duchess was making her first visit to an industrial estate since her marriage. The royal visit caused terrific excitement, and outside Ronuk there were 1,800 school-children plus a large crowd of residents. Two of the youngest Ronuk girls presented the Duchess with roses.

The guard of honour outside Ronuk was formed by the Portslade and district branch of the Royal British Legion. The Duke shook hands with Pte Vinter, who lost a leg in the war but still managed to march on crutches with his comrades. The royal couple was met by T.H. Fowler, director, P.W. Felton, director, and D.E. Sundius Smith, chairman of the council. Afterwards the Ronuk workers were given a half-day holiday and there was a party at the Ralli Hall.

This imposing building, which became Portslade Town Hall, was originally built for Ronuk as its Welfare Institute. It was opened in 1928. The hall even contained a splendid organ, made in 1885 by Michell & Thyne, and presented by Elizabeth Marion Chignall in memory of Robert Chignall, one of the first directors. There was also a billiard room, a spacious kitchen and separate recreation rooms for men and women.

The Ronuk workers took their lunch in the hall, with clean white tablecloths on each table and the floor waxed with the company's product, no doubt. Note the organ, and the collection of pictures on the walls, which were originals not prints. The pictures were donated by well-known artists of the time, such as Rex Vicat Cole and Byam Shaw. Mr Fowler knew many artists personally, dating back to the time when the Fowlers sold artist's materials.

These photographs show Ronuk girls at work in the 1950s. Note that the caps have long since gone. By this time Ronuk had diversified and several new products had been introduced, including Dirsof, a non-scratch cream, Colton, a wood dye, and Ronseal, which sealed the wood. There had also been boot polish (not a great success), Ronuk Carshine and Ronuk Carwax. The composition of the workforce was changing too, as there were a number of part-time women workers being employed. It is a far cry from the quantity of large tins on view here to the grave shortage of tin that the company suffered during both world wars. Indeed, so serious was the situation that Ronuk experimented with alternative packaging. Although the results may sound hilarious, sausage skins were given due consideration during the First World War, while grease-proof paper bags were favoured during the Second World War.

WAR

The most noticeable effect of the First World War on Portslade was the mushrooming of white bell tents on the playing fields of Windlesham House School. Naturally, this military camp proved a magnet for local children, especially when it became known that the soldiers could be generous with their rations. More than seventy years later, George Steele could still recall the marvellous taste of the Australian apricot jam he was given. After a bad storm the camp was flooded out and the soldiers were hastily billeted in the neighbourhood. Three soldiers arrived at the Steele home, but Mrs Steele was compensated for the inconvenience by being paid 1s a day for each soldier, plus extra rations.

At the beginning of the Second World War the south coast seemed a safe haven for London evacuees, and 1,176 of them arrived at Portslade. One of the first tasks was to take the children to a hall in Franklin Road, where their hair was fine combed and you could hear the lice dropping on to the newspapers spread over the floor. The evacuees placed a severe strain on schools, and children were taught in shifts in the classrooms, while others had lessons in the open air. However, their stay was short because, after Dunkirk, the area no longer seemed to be a secure retreat.

The 1st Field Company of the Royal Engineers pose gravely for their photograph, 1915. These men were quartered in the camp set up on Windlesham House's playing fields. It is quite probable that some of their training took place on the site where Vale Park is today. At that time it was full of waterlogged holes from which sand and flints had been extracted. The soldiers constructed bridges over them.

Some more soldiers from the camp, c. 1916. These men are grouped in the Locks Hill plantation where the children used to gather beech nuts. When the soldiers were billeted in private houses until huts were erected to replace the tents, pay-day was an interesting spectacle. The paymaster marched up the road accompanied by soldiers bearing a chair and folding table. These were plonked on the pavement and the soldiers lined up smartly. Later the camp became a military cookery instruction centre.

Portslade National Fire Service in 1941 outside the Southdown Motor Works in Victoria Road. Harry Flowers is seated in the front row, second from the left. In the background is the ladder belonging to the engine, which also boasted a Coventry Climax pump. Before the war the men were known as the Portslade Auxiliary Fire Service. In 1948 the County Fire Authority took over.

The 19th Platoon, 14th Battalion (Hove) Sussex Home Guard, 1943. In the second row, third from left, is Sgt Deacon. Fourth from the left is Lt Howard. They are outside what had been Windlesham House School. The Portslade Home Guard really did have a passing resemblance to *Dad's Army*. At least they were spared broom handles as they drilled with proper rifles, but these were cumbersome relics from the Boer War and sported a 16-inch bayonet.

The 14th Battalion (Hove) Sussex Home Guard, F Platoon, D Company. In the front row, third from left, is Sgt Field. Maj. Tyson, who lived in Lindfield House, was also part of this company. They were based at the brewery. Charlie Todd, who was in E Company of the same platoon, remembered one dark night on guard duty up on the Downs when the men feared that German paratroops had arrived on seeing hundreds of tiny lights. They were glow-worms.

A Civil Defence group outside warden post no. 8, which was at the foot of Applesham Way. In the second row, seated on the far left, is Florence Reed, who found romance in the Portslade Civil Defence in the shape of George Steele, whom she married in October 1948. There were also plenty of romances between the Canadian soldiers stationed in the area and Portslade girls. The first one to get married at St Nicolas's Church was a lance-corporal from the Calgary Highlanders.

With so much activity from the Home Guard, it was only natural that the children should want to emulate them. Besides, the Home Guard had their HQ just a few steps from the children's homes in North Road. This was the North Road Junior Home Guard, *c.* 1942. Front row, left to right: Sylvia Field, Bobby Nye and Dennis Field. Second row: Betty Miller, Jo Rochester and Colin Mills. Third row: Peter Miller and Peter Mills. Back row: Audrey Nye and Monty May.

A family at war, 1941. Back row, left to right: Charlie Todd (Home Guard), Muriel Todd (Land Army) and Jack Todd (regular Army). Front row: Evelyn Todd (London Fire Service) and Bessie Todd (Land Army). Their mother had a tough time bringing up the youngsters when their father died in 1925 as a result of being gassed in the First World War. The British Legion had to fight for her to receive a war widow's pension.

URBAN DISTRICT OF PORTSLADE-BY-SEA.

June, 1942.

COMPULSORY EVACUATION OF CHILDREN AND MOTHERS.

Arrangements are now being completed for those Mothers and Children who recently registered for Evacuation **in the event of this being ordered.**

NOTICE TO LEAVE MAY BE SHORT, AND YOU SHOULD THEREFORE MAKE ALL NECESSARY PREPARATIONS NOW.

Upon receiving notice, you must assemble with your children at the time stated in the notice, at the Recreation Ground Extension, Victoria Road, Portslade-by-Sea. If wet, shelter will be provided at the adjoining Garage of Southdown Motor Services, Limited.

You may only take with you such luggage as you can conveniently carry. Heavier Luggage and Prams will not be allowed on the train.

All luggage should be labelled with the name and home address of the owner.

Each person (Mother and Children) should take :
- (a) National Registration Identity Card.
- (b) Ration Book.
- (c) Gas Mask.
- (d) Rug or Blanket.
- (e) Knife, Fork, Spoon and Mug.
- (f) Food for 24 hours.
- (g) Change of Clothes.

Mothers should also take any Bank Book, Pensions Payment Order Book, Insurance Cards, and Insurance Policies (if any), Unemployment Book, Army Allowance Pay Book, and any ready money in their possession.

Accompanying this Notice is a label, with your name and those of your children on it who are registered for Evacuation. **THIS MUST BE WORN BY YOU AND TIED ON IN A VISIBLE POSITION.** It will admit you and your children to the train.

It is desirable that each child should be identified with a label, stating thereon his or her full name and home address, and separate labels for this purpose are sent herewith.

ERNEST H. KEMPE,
Clerk to the Council.

PLEASE READ THESE INSTRUCTIONS CAREFULLY, AND KEEP THEM BY YOU IN A SAFE PLACE FOR REFERENCE IF AND WHEN REQUIRED.

This document is evidence that fear of a German invasion was not confined to the few weeks after Dunkirk. Mothers and children were expected to hold themselves ready to leave at short notice. Of course, some children had already been evacuated, but this had been a voluntary scheme. For instance, some children from St Nicolas's School went to Sowerby Bridge in Yorkshire in 1941, and the boys from the Loxdale home went to Yorkshire too.

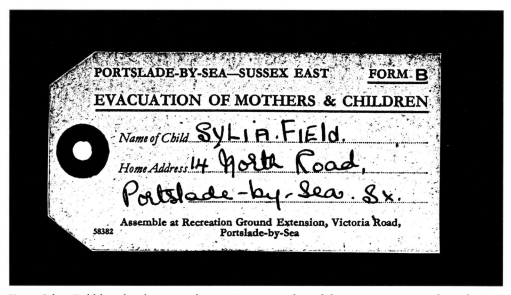

This label was for Kenneth Fuller, whose parents were married at St Nicolas's Church in 1924. A bill for their wedding cake is illustrated on p. 99. Kenneth's father, George Fuller, once worked for Baker's in North Street, where he had charge of a black horse called Captain, who was so large that young George had to stand on a box to throw a blanket over him.

Young Sylvia Field has already appeared on p. 67 as a member of the junior Home Guard. At the time when this ticket was issued, her mother was a member of the WVS Emergency Food and Shelter staff. She was also one of the main organizers of the North Road VE Party (p. 70).

The North Road VE Party in 1945, comprising about forty children and forty adults. There was a feast of sandwiches, sausage rolls, homemade cakes, jellies and blancmange. Then everyone went to the village green for races and games. Mrs Field was sad at losing an old family ring of emeralds and diamonds, which slipped off her finger in the excitement and was never seen again. Afterwards, it was back to North Road for ices, and each child was given a 3*d* bit.

There were other parties on VE day, and this is the happy group in Melrose Avenue. Altogether, Portslade had been extremely lucky during the Second World War because, although there were 1,036 air-raid alerts and thirty-six high-explosive bombs, not a single resident was killed. The war memorial tells a different story: forty-six men killed. However, this was nothing like the horrific toll of the First World War, when more than 600 Portslade men and one woman, Miss M.W. Gibbins, died.

ST ANDREW'S CHURCH

For centuries the population of Portslade was centred on the old village and its church of St Nicolas. However, during the early nineteenth century a community of people grew up in south Portslade, in the area around Wellington Road and North Street. This was known as Copperas Gap. Indeed, when the railway arrived in 1840 the station was called Copperas Gap rather than Portslade. The men earned their living at sea, on the canal or working in the brickfields. The Revd E.G. Holbrooke (vicar of Portslade 1859–80) instigated the building of St Andrew's Church to serve these people, and the church was dedicated on 18 October 1864. It remained a chapel of ease to St Nicolas's until 1876, when it became a separate parish.

Unusually, the church does not stand in its own graveyard, the reason being that the Revd William Hall refused to give his permission. He was the landowner who had donated the church site, and naturally people assumed that the Bishop of Chichester would soon consecrate the adjoining land. It proved to be an embarrassing hiatus in burial arrangements at Portslade because the churchyard at St Nicolas's was full and had been officially closed, so the deceased were buried at Aldrington or Hangleton until the matter was resolved. The Portslade Burial Board was constituted in 1871 to find an alternative burial ground.

This view of the church looking like a non-conformist chapel dates from the 1880s, when it was still a simple structure. It looks curiously isolated, as though it were miles away from any habitation. In fact it was anticipating further expansion in the area and its parish was already well populated in small streets to the south. The church cost £1,541 to build, and that included the boundary walls and gates.

The church proved to be so popular that in 1890 a north aisle was constructed at a cost of £911. It meant that the building could now hold a congregation of 525 people. Just visible to the left in this view of about 1900 is the imposing vicarage, which in 1881 was occupied by the vicar, the Revd Edward Winterbottom, his wife, son and two servants.

A peaceful scene, *c.* 1916 – the sheep grazing in the foreground add a pastoral touch. In the 1930s St Richard's Flats were built on this piece of ground and blessed by the Bishop of Lewes on 8 February 1936. It was a cold day with a bitter wind, so the service and address took place inside the church. Another service with a difference took place in May 1913: a church parade was held, and attended by the 6th (Cyclist) Battalion, Royal Sussex Regiment.

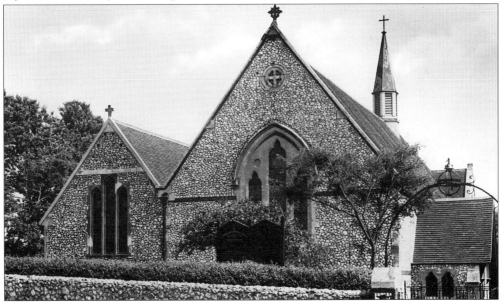

The church, 1950s. Between then and today the immediate surroundings of the church have undergone a dramatic change. The vicarage was demolished, and the Portslade Health Centre was built on the site and opened in 1982. The Catholic church of Our Lady, Star of the Sea, has also gone, being replaced by housing, while to the south the church hall has been replaced by a smart car showroom.

The interior of the church was originally quite plain and austere. Except for the coloured roundels in the east window, it had plain glass. However, prosperous patrons transformed the church into a wealth of stained glass, the most beautiful example being the two-light window designed by Edward Burne-Jones and made by Morris & Company, depicting St Wilfrid and St George. St Wilfrid is dressed in bishop's vestments with a background of deep blue and green.

The interior had changed considerably by the time of this view, *c.* 1915. The stone pulpit, which replaced the wooden one, is of particular interest as it was given in memory of Edward Thomas Booth, who died on 8 February 1890. Booth was the originator of the famous Booth Bird Museum at Brighton, but so far no connection with Portslade has come to light. His family moved to St Leonard's-on-Sea when he was young, and that is where he was buried.

SCHOOLS

The earliest type of education in Portslade was provided by Dame Schools: a small school run by a local woman who imparted the basics. In the 1770s there was a Dame School run by Dame Dod, a widow, who charged the Overseers of the Poor 7s 2d a year to educate young Fanny – obviously an orphan or illegitimate child. In the 1860s there was another Dame School run by Martha Mort, whose husband was the village baker. However, by this time there was a 'proper' school run by certificated teacher Gabriel McConnochie, and it made him hot under the collar when children on the way to the parochial school passed by Mrs Mort's and decided to go there instead.

The parochial school, the direct descendant of which is St Nicolas's School, was established in the village in about 1841. The site, donated by George Hall of Portslade House, was in the South Street area near Robin's Row. In 1872 the school moved to Locks Hill, where a new building had been provided by Hannah Brackenbury. At the official opening there was a splendid tea at which 50 large loaves, 200 lb of plum cake and 36 gallons of tea were consumed. The same decade also saw the creation of St Andrew's School, first in the North Street area and then moving to larger premises in Wellington Road.

St Nicolas's Girls School, *c*. 1907. In the back row, second from left, is Mrs Mary Florence Sayers, headmistress 1891–1927. The school had opened as a separate department in 1883 and the diocesan inspector enthused that it was 'an incalculable boon to the education of the children'. Mrs Sayers experienced the problem of juggling her career with motherhood, and in 1901 she had to take two weeks off because her daughter was ill with diphtheria.

St Nicolas's Boys School, *c*. 1907. Mr Robert Price, headmaster 1894–1922, is standing on the far left of the back row. Price was a bold man, for he had only been at the school a year when he asked the managers for a rise in salary because the average attendance of boys had gone up from 91 to 130. He was awarded a £12 increase, which brought his salary up to £132 a year.

St Nicolas's Girls School celebrates May Day in 1912, with Miss Terry and Mrs Sayers standing in the background. That same year Mrs Sayers completed twenty-five years service with the school, and there was a special presentation when everyone crowded into the school to see her receive a silver-plated tea and coffee service. Mrs Sayers had to adjust the curriculum in 1912 when the inspectorate decided that too much time was spent on domestic skills to the detriment of mental arithmetic.

St Nicolas's Infants School, *c.* 1918. Boys and girls were taught together in the infants department, housed in a new red-brick building opened in 1903 on the west side of Locks Hill. Front row, left to right: Harold Savage, ? Miles, Bob Partner, -?-, Fred Alderton, Ernie Redman and Bob Bennett.

St Nicolas's Girls School, *c.* 1912. The pupils are dressed as little Irish girls. Mrs Sayers is standing on the right wearing an elaborate hat. The teacher on the left is probably Miss Winifred Terry, who left in 1913 to be married. Marriage was a serious event and a young woman could not automatically expect to carry on teaching. For example, in 1898 Miss Edwards of the same department had to ask the manager's permission to retain her post after marriage.

St Nicolas's Girls School bazaar and sale of work, 4 June 1913. Mrs Sayers is on the left and her daughter Miss Elsie Sayers is on the right. Elsie hoped to follow in her mother's footsteps and she became a pupil teacher, but she could not finish her training because of illness. Instead she taught the girls gymnastics and Swedish drill, and undertook some voluntary work for the school.

St Nicolas's Boys School in 1924, photographed by Mr Pettit of North Street, Portslade. Front row, left to right: -?-, -?-, Jack Robinson, Ted Everest, Archie Greenyer, George Berry and Charlie Hickling. Second row, from the right: Fred Mack, Albert Peters and George Sizer. Third row, from the right: Ernie Redman, Fred Alderton and George Kelsey. In 1924 the school was in something of a crisis because no major repairs had been done since before the First World War and the inspectorate was not happy.

Class 2 of St Nicolas's School, 1926. It fell to the lot of a remarkable priest, the Revd Donald Campbell, to try to do something about the schools. He became vicar of Portslade in 1919 and it was a matter of raising sufficient money or handing over control to the State. Some people did not agree with his appeal in the first place: Ronuk, for instance, thought that church schools belonged to the past and council-run schools were better.

St Nicolas's Girls School stoolball team, 1928. Back row, left to right: Lily Neeve, Bessie Trigwell, Joyce Spooner, Gladys Neal and Lily Barnett. Second row: Peggy Miles, -?-, Miss Nunn, Doris Nutley and Freda Pyke. Front row: Kathleen Ford (Captain) and Doris Savage. In 1925 the stoolball team achieved a particularly satisfying score: St Nicolas 100, Patcham 41.

St Nicolas's School, 1930. John Broomfield is sitting on the far left and Betty Tidy is standing at the back. By 1930 the Revd Donald Campbell had left Portslade, soon to become Archdeacon of Carlisle, but not before he had turned the school's fortunes around. By October 1926, thousands of pounds had been raised and the necessary work had been done. There had been a large grant from the Diocesan Fund, but much of the money was raised locally.

St Nicolas's Boys School in 1932, with teacher Reg Figgins standing at the back. The boys moved to the old infants department in 1924. The headmaster was Mr J.W. Burn and the school earned the nickname of 'Burns Academy'. Burn was a northerner and he used to tell the children: 'You boys look as intelligent as a bunch of cows.' In 1927 there were 202 boys at the school, with four teachers and the headmaster.

A group from Portslade Senior Boys School outside the former Windlesham House school buildings, *c*. 1940. In 1929 there was a big shake-up in education at Portslade, with the boys from St Andrew's School joining those at St Nicolas's to become the Senior Boys School, while all of the girls were concentrated at the old St Andrew's School, which became the Senior Girls School. St Nicolas's and St Andrew's had a mixed junior and infant department each.

St Andrew's School, *c*. 1912. The original school was built in the 1870s in the North Street area, but reopened in 1881 in Wellington Road. It was enlarged in 1885 and 1894, and the building was completely gutted and rebuilt in 1914. The Bishop of Chichester reopened it on 25 April of that year. In 1908 there were strict instructions to the headmistress that, because of overcrowding, no girls from Fishersgate or Hove were to be admitted.

St Andrew's School in 1924, celebrating Empire Day. The school suffered considerably from its proximity to industry. In 1930 there was the noise of drilling as oil tanks were erected opposite the school, and there was a continuous problem with dust and grit from the power station. In July 1936 the headmistress complained bitterly that she was employed to teach and not to fish out grit from her pupils' eyes. It was painful for the children and sixty-five were affected.

St Winifred's School, 1920. These children were photographed in the field now occupied by St Richard's Flats. Reg Forrest is in the second row from the back on the far left. St Winifred's was a small private school and it existed on two sites: one in St Andrew's church hall and the other at 330 Portland Road, Hove. The Portslade school was the earlier one, and pupils were expected to pay 1s 6d first thing on Monday morning. The headmistress was Miss Lilian Herbert.

St Mary's Roman Catholic School, 1930s. Proposals for the school first appeared in 1913, but Hove Council bristled at the idea that pupils from Aldrington would be accepted when there was a perfectly good school in Portland Road. The promoters dropped Aldrington and the building went ahead. However, it had barely been completed when it was taken over for Belgian refugees, and it did not open as a school until 1918. It was paid for by Mrs Catherine Broderick.

The two photographs on this page, dating from the 1930s, show the buildings of Windlesham House, including the famous chapel. Windlesham House School claims to be the oldest purely preparatory school in the country, having been founded in 1837 by Lt C.R. Malden on the Isle of Wight. The school arrived at Portslade in 1913, the Maldens having purchased the beautiful Portslade House estate. The one stumbling block was the name of Portslade, popularly associated with gas works and other industrial concerns. Mrs Malden solved that by locating the school in Southern Cross, the name of a nearby pub.

This chapel (below) started life as the old Carfax church at Oxford. When it was demolished in 1896 it was purchased by Mrs Malden and erected at Brighton as the school chapel. When the school moved to Portslade it was taken down and re-erected, and when the school moved again in 1935 the operation was repeated.

The playing fields of Windlesham House, 1930s. The cricket field was prepared by laying turf from the old wicket area at Brighton. Thus the boys were playing on turf hallowed by seventy years of schoolboy cricket. There were many beech trees in the school grounds, and overlooking the cricket ground there were three special trees called the treble crossing. Only the best climbers could swing from tree to tree. Tree climbing was allowed on Sundays.

The library of Windlesham House. In the background there is a panel recording the names of sixty-six old boys who died in the First World War. The boys went on to public schools or the Naval College at Dartmouth, and the dormitories reflected the link, being named Harrow, Marlborough, Wellington, Rugby and Haileybury. The curriculum was strongly influenced by the requirements of the common entrance exam.

Windlesham House boasted its own swimming pool. The boys took a daily dip, and as the water was hardly ever changed it became progressively greener. One regular swimmer was the distinguished actor Sir Michael Hordern, who was known as Hordern 3 because his two older brothers also went there. He was at the school for nine years and he enjoyed it. He also felt that he received a good education.

A family group at Windlesham House, 1934. Christopher Scott Malden (headmaster (1927–53) and his wife Helen are seated, surrounded by their children. Bridget and Roger (headmaster 1953–58) are standing, and seated are Anthea and Charles (head with his wife Elizabeth Ann Malden from 1958 until the 1990s, when the school was sold). Charles was the great-great-grandson of the founder

The domestic staff of Windlesham House, *c.* 1914. In the back row, Mrs Turner is standing second from right, while in the front row, second from left, is Ellen Simmons. Known as Eli, she worked mainly as a matron and stayed at the school for more than forty years. Next to her in the place of most importance is the no-nonsense figure of the cook. There were between fifty and sixty hungry boys to cater for, as well as the staff.

Domestic staff, *c.* 1924. This picture shows how ten years have altered things. The First World War changed the domestic situation completely, as young girls were given the opportunity to earn higher wages in factories or doing other war work. The days of the starched apron and frilly cap were over. Some faces can still be recognized – Mrs Turner (third from left, back row), and the cook and Eli have swapped places in the middle row.

This school was known in the early days as the Portslade Industrial School, but was really an approved school constructed jointly by the London County Council and Brighton Council in 1902 at a cost of £30,000. It was certainly no holiday camp, and the boys followed a tough regime, which included cold showers and daily scrubbing of the floors with more cold water. As the school was built on an exposed site, there was an abundance of fresh air too.

Like contemporary public schools, discipline was enforced by six of the best at the least provocation. At Portslade the head had a habit of walking away first, so that he could get a good run-up to his unfortunate target. Another punishment was to be deprived of the Saturday night film show and a handful of sweets. The victim had to sit out in the cold corridor while his friends enjoyed themselves.

STREETS, SHOPS & TRADE

Two features that are noticeable on looking at old photographs are the lack of traffic and the appearance of self-sufficiency. People's needs were few and could be met locally. Shops in the village, like Read's Supply Stores, provided a variety of goods; bread was baked locally; and dairy produce and vegetables were close at hand. The pubs, school and church were all within easy walking distance.

In south Portslade the main shopping area was North Street, where the shops really were open all hours. The street also contained several butchers, one of which had its own slaughteryard at the rear. The animals arrived by rail and were driven down Station Road, and this practice continued until the 1930s. On one occasion a bull escaped and charged into an estate agent's office (Young, Holbech & Sadler), bellowing at the terrified employees who cowered behind the counter. In earlier days Mr Hardy, pork butcher of North Street, caused a sensation by becoming the first person in the area to have electric light. This was provided by a gas engine that drove Hardy's own dynamo.

The road was named after the Battle of Trafalgar pub, which pre-dated the houses and shops built at various dates. Indeed, when the pub was erected, probably in the 1860s, it stood on its own with a small piece of land in front, which was acquired in 1903 to make the road wider. This photograph of Trafalgar Road was taken in about 1905 and shows Coustick's bakery on the corner with Coustick's horse and cart in front of the fir trees.

Trafalgar Road in 1910, with W. Coustick's shop still prominent. Coustick also ran the Southern Cross post office. Next door to him was a furniture shop run by Mr Peters. In view of the trees it is not surprising that no. 81 was called The Firs. Another appropriate name used to belong to the houses next to the Southern Cross Mission, which in the 1890s were known as Nelson Terrace.

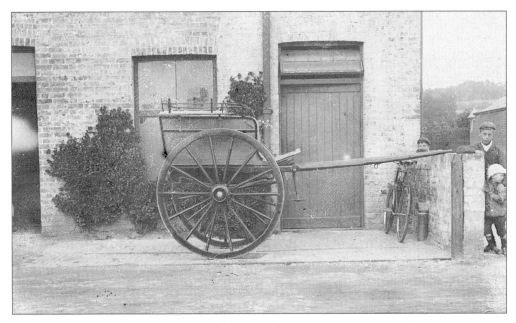

Coustick's bakery was on the corner of Trafalgar Road and Victoria Road. Here, three young Coustick brothers are at the back of the premises with a rather elegant trap, but no pony. Later on, Hector and John Coustick were to sing in the choir at St Nicolas's Church.

Aldrington Dairies at 90 Trafalgar Road was run by William Alfred Sears in the 1930s. Here he is standing in the doorway next to the trade bike. During the Second World War, most of the roundsmen were called up, so Aldrington Dairies had to employ females, nicknamed, of course, the 'milkmaids'. It was hard work, involving two deliveries a day, seven days a week, plus bottling the milk and cleaning the bottles at the end of the day.

Above: Time for a quiet chat in an almost traffic-free Church Road, 1930s. On the corner with the blind drawn down is B. Young's shop. Next door to him is C. Pengilly's cobblers shop, which business dated back to 1908. Pengilly was a skilled craftsman, but he also sold pieces of leather so that hard-up dads could mend their own sons' boots. Next door was Maugham's the newsagent where tobacco and snuff were sold by the ounce.

Left: The Cricketer's inn in Church Road was taken over by Tamplin's in 1892. The indomitable lady standing outside is probably Mrs Sarah Ann Wickens, who ran the pub in the 1890s and into Edwardian times. This part of Portslade was once plentifully endowed with pubs, but while the old rivals in North Street and the Crown inn in Wellington Road have long since closed their doors, the Cricketer's remains.

It will no doubt come as a surprise to many Portslade people that Burton's bakery, photographed *c.* 1900, still exists though it is now much altered. The building is to be found in Romany Close, and there are those who say that the scent of freshly baked bread can still be detected occasionally. The business was started in the 1890s as the Hygienic Bakery by Charles Burton, who later sold it to his brother, George Burton.

Burton's bakery delivered its bread with the help of these two handcarts. The large oven was at the back of the premises and, as a service to his customers, George Burton would bake Christmas cakes and cook Christmas dinners for 2*d* and 3*d* a time. The bakery had a hoist, which swung the large bags of flour on to the top floor.

The Petersfield laundry in Old Shoreham Road, pictured here in 1907, was run by Arthur Wellesley Green. The business was established in 1879 and new works opened in 1896. At this time the laundry was advertised as the 'only Gold Medallist in the County for Shirt Dressing'. Its employees were also experts with ball dresses, and every description of fancy goods could be cleaned with the 'dry process without unpicking'.

Another well-known laundry was run by Alfred Tate, pictured here in about 1906. The roof advertisement proclaims 'good open drying ground', which was where Foredown Drive is today. Tate's laundry was on the corner of Old Shoreham Road. Almost as a sideline, the Tates started a little engineering works at the back of the laundry — they had a reputation for understanding cars ever since Alfred Tate joined the Emancipation Run in 1896.

The next move by the Tate family was to open their first garage at Southern Cross in 1929, a modest single-storey building with two hand-operated pumps serving petrol over the pavement. It was a corner site. In fact, as anyone who knows Portslade will recognize, the Tates seemed to specialize in acquiring corner sites. Here, Jack Westbrook is pictured beside the pumps, *c.* 1934

This was Tate's Garage in 1954, with a few more petrol pumps on the forecourt. In that year the old laundry building was lost in a fire, but the Tates had other interests too. For instance, during the Second World War they ran a salvage and repair business for boats and designed gun-depression gear for use on the well-known Oerlikon guns mounted on many ships of the Royal Navy. After the war they designed and manufactured equipment for overhead power lines.

The bus drawn up outside Portslade railway station looks somewhat uncomfortable and even unstable, but perhaps that is because the lady trying to descend the staircase seems tall in comparison with the small figure of the driver. This bus route saw some interesting changes. The early Milnes-Daimler motor buses used it, but after complaints about excessive noise, electrobuses were tried out. These had electric rechargeable batteries that weighed about 30 cwt.

Portslade railway station, 1920s. The original station was west of the level-crossing and was opened on 12 May 1840. It was resited to its present position in 1881. In 1911 the sanitary inspector was horrified to discover that the station still had its own cesspool in the garden. He ordered it to be filled in and the drain connected to the Portland Road sewer.

Right: This view dates from *c*. 1923 and shows the original shop of A. Pierce & Son at 25 Station Road. The family lived next door and in 1927 Pierce extended the shop by knocking out the front room of the family's house, thus creating a double-fronted premises. The Pierces ran an ironmongery, which sold everything from dustbins (price 7*s* 6*d*) to tin baths. They also mixed up paint for their customers which included linseed oil and white lead.

Below: By 1929 Mr Pierce had purchased two houses in Boundary Road, Hove, opposite his old shop. At that time there were few shops in the road but many private houses. Pierce then set about building two shops where the front gardens had been. This is how that shop window at 58 Boundary Road looked in 1937, decorated patriotically in honour of the coronation.

A procession to celebrate the coronation in 1911 moves slowly down Station Road/Boundary Road. This road has certainly seen a few name changes. In the past the track was known as Aldrington Lane or Red House Droveway, and by the 1880s it was Aldrington Drove. Soon it was Station Road on both sides, until 1903, when Hove decided to change its side to Boundary Road. This photograph was taken by Mr Tubb, whose premises were in Boundary Road.

For those who are familiar with Station Road/Boundary Road today, there is only one word to describe this scene of past days, and that is 'tranquil'. Note also the elegant houses on the Portslade side. They were called Courtney Terrace (probably after the middle name of a previous landowner), and the largest was Courtney House, where the Sundius Smith family lived, owners of the Britannia flour mills. The shops opposite were grandly called The Parade.

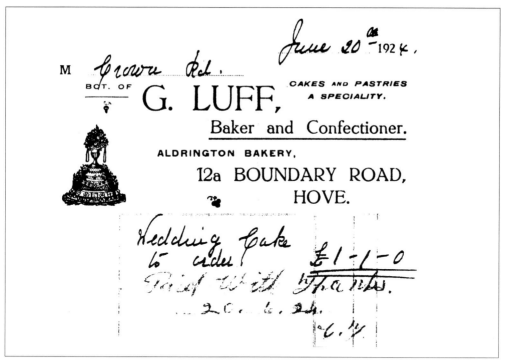

Mr and Mrs George Fuller were married at St Nicolas's Church in 1924, and this was the bill for their wedding cake from the Aldrington Bakery, which came to one guinea. George was working for Hillman's the contractor at the time. He took the Saturday off for the wedding but he had to lose the money. The young couple was too hard up to be able to afford a photographer, never mind a honeymoon.

When this photograph is shown as a slide at lectures, it arouses more comment than any other shot of Portslade. Thus it is obvious that the Co-op is remembered with some affection. Many old Portslade residents can remember their Co-op number as readily as soldiers can recall their service number. At every transaction the customer's number was noted and people looked forward to the annual divi-day, when there was always a long queue. This handsome building was replaced by a nondescript edifice put up for the Post Office.

North Street, *c.* 1908. At this time the road was still lined with small shops and businesses. The familiar name of the undertakers, Baker & Sons, started here in a small way and was run by three generations of the family. In the early days nobody could earn a living from funerals alone, so the family also ran a forge and operated a profitable sideline providing crushed stone for roadworks.

North Street, 1940s. On the right is the Salvation Army Hall and beyond it is H. Baker, timber importers (a separate concern from the undertakers). On the left is the twin-towered Baptist Church, with the Pavilion cinema in the foreground. The cinema was rebuilt by Percy Victor Reynolds and reopened in 1932. He managed to squeeze in 600 seats, so there was not much leg room but the seats were beautifully upholstered in emerald green, while the screen was elegant in festoon curtains of grey velvet.

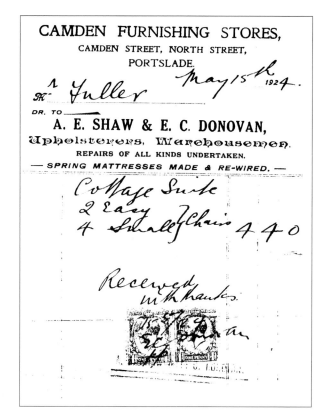

The bill for chairs was for the same young couple whose wedding cake bill was featured on p. 99. This was a large sum of money to pay out. Quite often in those days a couple would have a long engagement so that they could save up for a few sticks of furniture. It was also often the case that you could not take the furniture home until the last instalment had been paid.

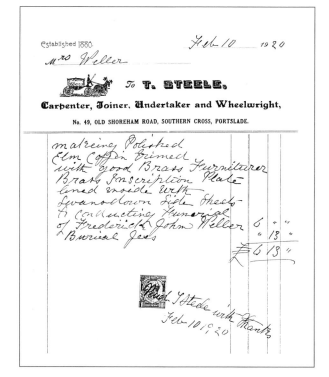

T. Steele's business was established in 1880, and in 1920 his premises were at 49 Old Shoreham Road. Similar to Baker's in the early days, he had other strings to his bow: carpenter, joiner and wheelwright. In those days the importance of a funeral was gauged by the number of horses employed. A really grand send-off required four horses (with sable plumes, no doubt). Needless to say, the one-horse variety was the most common at Portslade.

A general view of the fitters' space at the Southdown Motor Works in Victoria Road, 31 August 1928. By 1936, Southdown owned 670 vehicles and employed 200 people to service them here. They included engineers, painters, electricians, upholsterers and signwriters, and there was also a clothing store to dispense uniforms to bus drivers and conductors. The vehicles were all Tilling-Stevens or Leyland buses.

Cecil Peters standing in front of the garage in Victoria Road, owned by the Russel Brothers, where he became an apprentice mechanic in 1929, aged fourteen. The Austin 12 (GX 4366) belonged to Mr Beck, who kept pigs at Mile Oak. The garage was prepared to mend virtually anything, and that included propellers for the boats in the harbour.

PEOPLE

It is strange that the population of neighbouring parishes like Hove and Portslade should have been so different. The crucial fact was that Hove was virtually a Victorian creation, and therefore many of its inhabitants had been born elsewhere, whereas at Portslade some families had been established for generations.

One such family were the Peters, who were at Portslade at least by the eighteenth century. In 1852 there were twenty-two tradesmen in the village, of whom seven were Peters. They were millers, a butcher, a baker, a landlord, a letter carrier and a collector of taxes. Later they branched out into farming and market gardening. They formed a web of relationships by marrying into other well-known local families, such as the Cheesmans, the Patchings and the Steeles.

However, the prize for the longest association with Portslade must go to the Blaker family. Edward Blaker of Portslade was assessed for tax in 1553 and the family continued to live in the village until this century, the last representative dying at St Helen's in the 1960s. They allied themselves to other families of wealth in the area. For example, in 1864 John Blaker married Mary Borrer, whose family home was Portslade Manor, while the Borrers were related to the Hall family, who owned Portslade House.

Harry Peters, pictured here in the 1890s, spent most of his life in Alma Cottage. In the 1860s he lived there with Abraham Peters (probably his brother), plus Abraham's wife and eight children. Both men earned their living as market gardeners. Alma Cottage was probably built for the Peters family in the 1850s, no doubt soon after the glorious battle of the Alma (20 September 1854), the first battle of the Crimean War where the British and French were victorious.

Outside a house in Abinger Road, near the corner of Gardner Street, *c*. 1898. On the right is Tom Peters and on the left is his son, also Tom, and his daughter Dolly. The younger man was the landlord of the nearby Gardner's Arms. According to the directory, a Thomas Peters was also landlord of the Southern Cross pub in 1887.

Mrs G. Tate Forrest sitting stolid and unsmiling, nursing on her knee young 'Pop' Forrest, in Portslade, 1892. She was the great-grandmother of Reg Forrest, who used to run the barber's shop next door to Tate's Garage at Southern Cross. Reg was also one of those Portslade children who watched E.G. Miles building his plane at the Star laundry next to St Andrew's School, which he attended.

This portrait of Marianne Stallabrass in the 1890s shows a woman of independence and industry. She took the highly unconventional step of leaving her husband behind in Hertford and decamping to Portslade with her three children. She bought and managed Portslade Farm, and lived in a colonial-style house with verandahs all round, called Hill Brow. Her son, Dennis, was famous in local annals for owning the first motor-car in Portslade.

Hector Coustick and his sister, sitting in a little handcart, *c.* 1902. Although the children kept quite still for the photographer, the dog could not and so his head is blurred. Note the wide-brimmed straw hat worn by Hector, which looks almost identical to the one worn by young Forrest on p. 105. It demonstrates that children's fashions did not change very quickly.

George Fuller, *c.* 1914. Like many of his contemporaries, Fuller left school at thirteen and his first job, helping to deliver furniture by means of a horse-drawn van, earned him 6*s* a week. He saw the transition from horse to motor transport and in the 1920s, when he was working for Baker's, he was despatched to the post office with 5*s* to buy a driving licence – no test needed.

Sam Underhill sports a magnificent drooping moustache in this portrait, featuring him wearing the regalia of Master of the Foresters' Friendly Society. The Portslade branch of the Foresters met at the old Crown inn, and in the nineteenth century it boasted the fifth highest membership in Sussex. Underhill once worked as a coachman for the vicar of St Nicolas before being employed at Britannia flour mills for many years. He died on Christmas Day 1943, aged seventy-two.

Miss Ethel Patching, a teacher at St Andrew's School, *c.* 1911. By 1921 Ethel was teaching at St Nicolas's Boys School. After the reorganization of 1929 she transferred to the junior and infants department. Her sisters, Annie and Hettie, kept a grocery shop at Southern Cross and were famous for the quality of their sausages. There are four tombstones to the Patching family in St Nicolas's churchyard.

Left: George Burton was a man of many talents. His bakery was featured on p. 93, and here he is in another role: champion shot. He used to practise in an indoor shooting range behind Franklin Road. Later he sold the bakery and set up a small engineering works in Vale Road. He was also an inventor, but the family wish that he had hung on to a patent that he sold to Cadbury's for £300: a device for stopping chocolate powder blowing over the machinery.

Below: George Burton, his wife and his son seated in a somewhat peculiar tricycle. Burton married Sarah in 1901 and spent many hours beforehand on his masterpiece, a tiered wedding cake weighing 96 lb embellished with latticework in almond icing. All of his customers received a slice. Another of his inventions was Burton's Patent Empire War Game, for which he made all of the lead soldiers, which his family helped to paint.

Daisy Blaber and Jack Tidy, photographed in the 1920s by H.W. Tubb. They both worked at the Petersfield laundry (p. 94). Jack had returned from war service with the Horse Artillery with both eardrums shattered by the noise of exploding shells. His mother assumed that he would never be able to do an ordinary job again, but he was determined to get back his job as a maintenance engineer – and he did.

George William Ring holds the bridle while his mother sits in the family trap in Crown Road, c. 1924. The stable was in Stanley Road. Ring was a builder and plasterer, specializing in delicate frieze work. He used the pony and trap to transport his materials. In 1934 he married Winifred, whose first job on leaving school at fourteen was working in Petersfield's laundry.

Sidney Chappell served with the Royal Sussex Regiment, having joined the 1st Battalion in 1905. He saw service in Malta, Crete, Belfast and India, and when he returned from the latter he brought a fine shawl and a parrot, which he taught to speak. He was killed at Vendresse, France, on 14 September 1914, and his name is recorded on the war memorial at Easthill Park.

A family portrait taken in 1916 by H.W. Tubb. This picture shows Charles Ernest Forrest and his wife Charlotte Mary, with their son Reg standing on a chair. Note that it was still fashionable to dress little boys in skirts at this age. Forrest is wearing the uniform of the Royal Garrison Artillery.

Alfred Ford, who served with the Royal
Engineers, and his wife Lucy with their
children, 1917. Ethel, Harry and Edith are
standing at the back, while Kathleen and Sid
are in front. The Ford's sixth child was born in
1920, but Mrs Ford died soon afterwards. Poor
Edith, who was only nineteen, had to leave her
job to bring up the children, including a six-
week old baby. Strangers, seeing a baby but no
wedding ring, looked at her with contempt.

George Ellis with his wife and daughter
Barbara, 1939. Ellis joined the 10th Army Field
Workshop, which was stationed at the brewery
in the village. As he was officially billeted it
meant that he was paid 6d a night to sleep in his
own bed. However, in March 1940 his unit was
shipped to France on board the *Ben Macree*. The
commanding officer, Capt. Caffyn, came into
his own at the Dunkirk evacuation because he
knew the area well and got his men safely to
Brest.

Mrs Amy Broomfield and her daughter, also called Amy, *c*. 1942. Amy junior had a twin brother called Albert and two other brothers, Maurice and Frank. Frank died in 1920 from injuries sustained in the First World War. All the Broomfields worked hard on their farm, but Amy was also an independent spirit. She had been a Land Girl in the First World War. Then in the 1930s she went skiing in Switzerland and took a luxury cruise to Buenos Aires.

Bert Hyde at North House Farm, 1950s. Hyde is at the wheel of a Massey Ferguson tractor – a far cry from the hand-milking he had done in the 1930s when he first went to work for John Broomfield. Hyde remained for forty years and worked for three generations of Broomfields. For many years he and his wife Gladys lived in a tied cottage at 31 High Street between the George and the Stag. Electricity was not installed until the 1950s.

Syd Baker, undertaker's assistant, *c*. 1929.
Note the silk top hat, obligatory wear but a
nuisance to keep looking good, particularly if
it rained at a funeral. Funerals were
traditionally held on Saturdays, so that those
attending did not lose wages. Syd was born
over the shop at 51 North Street. He grew up
surrounded by coffins and thought nothing of
playing hide and seek in them.

On the clinker dump of the electricity works A
station, *c*. 1927. George Masters is on the left.
Masters and Smelt were partners for a few
years, owning one lorry each, and the business
was run from 15 St Nicholas Road. Masters
spent three years with the Army Service Corps,
Sussex Yeomanry during the First World War,
and that is where he learned to drive motor
vehicles. He was invalided out of the Army
with rheumatic fever.

The Portslade Swifts Football Club for the 1919/20 season. By 1923 the club had ceased to exist, but there were seven other clubs at Portslade, including the gas works team and Portslade Wednesday. In October 1907 there was a disturbance at Victoria Recreation Ground over a penalty kick in the match between Portslade Wednesday and Aldrington Wednesday. The council sternly decreed that, if there was a future disturbance, it would reconsider giving them permission to play.

Four generations of the Packham family at Kemps, 1930s. Back row, left to right: Arthur Packham (police sergeant at Ditchling for many years), Philip Packham and Alfred Packham. Front row: Mrs Arthur Packham, Mrs Philip Packham (with Arthur's son Brian) and Mrs Alfred Packham. Philip Packham was born in the old cottages at North House Farm and served in windjammers for some years, before becoming head brewer at the Portslade brewery.

SECTION TWELVE

BUILDINGS

It is only in recent times that some of the old buildings at Portslade have acquired a wider appreciation, and it must be said that Portslade's reputation has suffered from the industrialization at the sea end. An example of this appears in a guide book of the 1920s, which famously advised travellers to hasten past the ugly houses of Portslade. Presumably the writer had never ventured north of the Old Shoreham Road. It is also a fact that some of the houses have survived precisely because the area was not fashionable. In 1974 Portslade village was made a conservation area and Hove Council have carried out a number of improvements, such as removing the festoons of telephone wires and creating red-brick pavements.

In the nineteenth century, Portslade contained a greater social mixture than it does today. The Borrer family, who owned a great deal of land at Portslade, lived at the manor; the Blakers lived at Easthill House; and the Mews brothers, who had made their money from brewing, built Whychote and Loxdale. These wealthy families were a great benefit to the village and could be relied on to support church and school, as well as providing practical help in other ways. When these families began to move away from the area, the village definitely felt the draught.

The manor ruins viewed from the convent grounds in 1973. Prominent in the background is the wall containing the thirteenth-century window, which was taken down in 1986 when it was found to be in a dangerous state. This picture gives a good idea of how overgrown the ruins were with swathes of ivy and sycamore trees. The trees were cut down in March 1992 and excavation started with the help of a grant from English Heritage.

Portslade folk were amazed to hear that the old neglected ruin was deemed to be of national importance. There are not many examples of Norman manor houses, so it is now scheduled as an ancient monument and a Grade II listed building. In this view, note the dark L-shaped (turned sideways) aperture because underneath is a piece of honeysuckle moulding, part of a decorative frieze that embellished the ground-floor room. In 1936 the date 1611 was also visible on the frieze.

The earliest part of the manor was built in the twelfth century, but there were alterations and extensions over the years. This view of 1995 shows the same piece of wall as in the picture opposite, but without the window. Since then the window has been restored to its old position. This picture also gives a good impression of how close together the church and manor were built. The manor was opened to the public on 17 March 1995.

The old manor was inhabited until 1807, when the new one, shown here in the 1880s, was built. On the left is a folly built from flints taken from the ruins. It is said that the old manor was used as an almshouse, but then it was destroyed. The great mystery is why this was done. Evidence shows that the building was not allowed to moulder away quietly; instead the walls were thrown down with some violence.

The beautiful and elegant mansion known as Portslade House, 1880s. This was probably built in the 1790s, when Nathaniel Hall purchased the estate and the Hall family became one of the principal landowners at Portslade. They had ceased to live in the house by the 1860s, preferring to rent it out. In 1871 it was occupied by Frederick R.M. Gosset, retired officer of the Bengal Army, his wife, six children and eight servants.

Whychote viewed from the garden side, 1938. This house was built for Herbert Mews of the Portslade brewery family and was capacious to say the least, with its nine bedrooms and two reception rooms. It was a typical Victorian extravaganza with its gables and prominent chimneys. It overlooks the village green, which until the 1930s was still a private field belonging to Whychote, with a public right of way running across the corner.

In 1928 Whychote was purchased by Andrew Melville, the owner of the Grand Theatre, North Road, Brighton. Here, Melville's second wife and their son John are sitting on the lawn with the old cottages in the High Street in the background. At one time this was the site of Hangleton Court, but over the years the Mews family bought plots of land and gradually extended the grounds around the house.

Andrew Melville was a member of Portslade Council, and at one stage its chairman. He died suddenly at the age of fifty-four in 1938, so Whychote had to be sold. This photograph of the lounge as well as the one opposite were included in the sale brochure. The house was sold for £10,000 to F.W.A. Cushman, who had been Mayor of Hove (1919–22). Cushman was proud of his garden and particularly of his President Hoover rose tree.

Loxdale was built for Walter Mews, the other partner in the brewery business. The plans, passed in 1899, were by Samuel Denman, a well-known local architect who was also responsible for the Portslade brewery and the imposing Hove Club in Fourth Avenue. Walter was fond of mahogany, a great deal of his furniture being composed of the wood, including a roll-top writing bureau, a long-case striking clock and two suites of dining chairs.

PORTSLADE CARNIVAL. "LOXDALE" MAY·26·1920

This carnival, held in the gardens of Loxdale on 26 May 1920, was in aid of St Nicolas's Church funds, and between 3,000 and 4,000 people attended. The two Mrs Mews were the hosts, assisted by an army of volunteers to help with the stalls and entertainments. Among the sports were a slow bicycle race and a cigarette lighting race. After supper there was dancing on the lawn until dusk, with music provided by the St John's Brass and Reed Band.

Portslade Lodge was built in about 1785 in typical Regency fashion, with bow front and verandah. It was first mentioned in 1789, when it was given to Mary Bull as part of her marriage settlement. The property included 5 acres of land, which in later years included a formal garden with shady walks, fruit trees and a heated vinery with sturdy vines. The house contained eight bedrooms and dressing rooms, and the drawing room was 23 feet by 20 feet, with french casements opening on to the verandah.

Sellaby House was built in the 1870s and purchased for Miss Alice King, the former companion of wealthy Hannah Brackenbury, who had recently died. Provision was made in her will for a villa to be bought for Miss King, who named it Sellaby House as a tribute to her employer, whose family had ancient connections with Selaby in County Durham. The downstairs room on the right was probably the drawing room, with windows to the east and south and a white marble fireplace.

A snow scene at St Helen's, 33 Mile Oak Road, 1934. This house was opened as a rest home in 1947 by Mr and Mrs G.D. Neild. Mrs Neild was the great-granddaughter of Charles Darwin. One of their residents was Joyce, daughter of Cecil Renshaw Blaker, and the last Blaker to live in Portslade. She died at St Helen's at the age of seventy-nine. Previously the house had been the sanatorium of Windlesham House School.

The fire station was opened in May 1909 by Walter Hillman, chairman of the council, wielding a massive silver key. The ceremony was attended by visiting firemen, including Superintendent Lacroix from Brighton and Capt. Dumbrell from Hove, as well as others from Haywards Heath and Eastbourne. The guests were treated to a substantial meat tea in the parish room. The building is a dramatic exercise in white brick and terracotta, designed by Portslade surveyor A. Taylor Allen and built by Mr E. Clevett.

Copperas Gap windmill used to stand on the corner of West Street and North Street. In 1813, during a violent storm, the young miller, William Huggett, was severely burned when lightning struck. However, he survived and remained miller for a number of years. In 1841 one of the two millers was John Bodle, and in later times his widow ran the Crown inn. The windmill was demolished in the 1870s.

This beautiful picture of East Hill windmill was painted by Frederick Nash in 1841. Francis Cheesman, miller, who died in 1746, was a man in comfortable circumstances owning a number of brass and pewter utensils, as well as four valuable feather beds, the chief one having numerous sets of sheets to go with it. His descendant, Susanna, married into the Peters family. Thomas Peters was miller in 1841 and he was also the man who made sure that Portslade's census returns were correctly recorded.

Our Lady, Star of the Sea, and St Denis was officially opened on 28 July 1912. Although the exterior was utilitarian, the inside was spectacular. The baldachin was made of wood by Mr Fonteneau, who lived in the parish. He was nearly seventy years old and originally came from Brittany. It was painted blue, red and gold. The chancel screen was made by George Greed to a design produced by Father Kerwin, who had been inspired by a screen he had seen in an Italian church while on a walking holiday.

The original Church of the Good Shepherd, Stanley Avenue, was erected on plots 37 and 38 of the former Paddocks Estate and was opened by the Bishop of Lewes on 8 November 1936. The building was donated by the vicar of the Good Shepherd, Brighton, and Mrs Gerald Moor. When the building was in the process of being put up, a gale threw the lot to the ground. During the Second World War it was also used as classrooms by a girls' school evacuated from London.

The new Church of the Good Shepherd was built as part of the Sussex Church Campaign and it was opened on 28 October 1967 by Dr Roger Wilson, Bishop of Chichester. It cost £25,000, of which All Saints', Hove, donated £7,500 and St Nicolas', Portslade, £2,000. It was a true child of the 1960s: innovative, optimistic and controversial. The striking modern stained glass was designed by Kenneth Budd.

ACKNOWLEDGEMENTS

The author would like to thank the following people and organizations for kindly loaning their photographs:

Brighton and Hove Libraries
Hove Borough Council (p. 14 top)
Hove Museum (p. 8 top, p. 208 bottom)
Royal Air Force Museum (p. 55 bottom)

Mr Syd Baker, Mrs Gladys Banfield, Mr John Broomfield, Mrs Dolle, the late Mr George Ellis, Mrs Field, Mrs Betty Figg, Mr H.G.J. Flowers, the late Mr Reg Forrest, the late Mr George Fuller, Mrs Dorothy Gedye, Mrs J. Hayward, Mr Michael Horscroft, Miss Avril Hunt, Mr Bert Hyde, the late Mr Fred Mack, Mr Charles Malden, Mrs Marriott, Mr Eric Masters, Mr John Melville, Mrs Neild, Mr Alan Osborne, Mr Cecil Peters, the late Mr Bert Pierce, the late Mr Ernie Redman, Mr Bill Ring, the Revd Richard Rushforth, Mr Sears, Mrs Smith, Mr G. Steele, Mr John Tate, the late Mr Charlie Todd, the late Mr George Webb and Mr Denis Williams.

BRITAIN IN OLD PHOTOGRAPHS

To order any of these titles please telephone our distributor, Littlehampton Book Services on 01903 721596
For a catalogue of these and our other titles please ring Regina Schinner on 01453 731114